50 Delicious Blender Recipes for Home

By: Kelly Johnson

Table of Contents

- Banana Smoothie
- Strawberry Banana Smoothie
- Mango Pineapple Smoothie
- Blueberry Almond Smoothie
- Green Detox Smoothie
- Avocado Cilantro Lime Dressing
- Classic Hummus
- Spicy Roasted Red Pepper Hummus
- Creamy Tomato Basil Soup
- Butternut Squash Soup
- Spicy Carrot Soup
- Vegan Creamy Mushroom Soup
- Chocolate Peanut Butter Milkshake
- Vanilla Almond Protein Shake
- Berry Oatmeal Smoothie
- Pineapple Coconut Smoothie
- Kale Pineapple Smoothie
- Apple Cinnamon Smoothie
- Sweet Potato Pie Smoothie
- Greek Yogurt Pancake Batter
- Easy Blender Salsa
- Roasted Tomato Sauce
- Cashew Cheese Sauce
- Classic Guacamole
- Cilantro Lime Rice
- Vegan Alfredo Sauce
- Smoothie Bowl Base
- Vegan Creamy Caesar Dressing
- Healthy Strawberry Shortcake Smoothie
- Spiced Pumpkin Smoothie
- Blackberry Chia Seed Smoothie
- Chocolate Avocado Pudding

- Vegan Ice Cream Base
- Mango Lassi
- Beet Apple Smoothie
- Mint Chocolate Chip Smoothie
- Pineapple Mint Smoothie
- Creamy Avocado Cilantro Dressing
- Sweet Green Smoothie
- Apple Ginger Smoothie
- Pear Spinach Smoothie
- Creamy Zucchini Soup
- Tomato Avocado Salsa
- Raspberry Lemon Smoothie
- Cucumber Melon Smoothie
- Peanut Butter Banana Protein Shake
- Cauliflower Rice
- Cilantro Avocado Smoothie
- Green Apple Kale Smoothie
- Pumpkin Spice Smoothie

Banana Smoothie

Ingredients:

- 2 ripe bananas
- 1 cup of milk (dairy or non-dairy, like almond or oat milk)
- 1/2 cup of Greek yogurt (optional for extra creaminess)
- 1 tablespoon of honey or maple syrup (adjust to taste)
- 1/2 teaspoon of vanilla extract (optional)
- 1/2 cup of ice cubes (for a chilled smoothie)

Instructions:

1. **Prepare the Bananas:** Peel the bananas and break them into chunks.
2. **Blend:** In a blender, combine the banana chunks, milk, Greek yogurt (if using), honey or maple syrup, and vanilla extract (if using).
3. **Add Ice:** Add the ice cubes if you want a cooler, thicker smoothie.
4. **Blend Until Smooth:** Blend on high until the mixture is smooth and creamy. If it's too thick, you can add a bit more milk to reach your desired consistency.
5. **Taste and Adjust:** Taste the smoothie and adjust sweetness or add more milk if needed.
6. **Serve:** Pour into glasses and enjoy immediately!

Feel free to add extras like a handful of spinach for a green smoothie, a spoonful of peanut butter for extra protein, or a sprinkle of cinnamon for added flavor.

Strawberry Banana Smoothie

Ingredients:

- 1 cup fresh or frozen strawberries
- 2 ripe bananas
- 1 cup milk (dairy or non-dairy, such as almond or soy milk)
- 1/2 cup Greek yogurt (optional for added creaminess)
- 1 tablespoon honey or maple syrup (optional, adjust to taste)
- 1/2 teaspoon vanilla extract (optional)
- 1/2 cup ice cubes (if using fresh strawberries and for a colder smoothie)

Instructions:

1. **Prepare the Fruit:** If you're using fresh strawberries, wash and hull them. Peel the bananas and break them into chunks.
2. **Blend:** In a blender, combine the strawberries, bananas, milk, Greek yogurt (if using), honey or maple syrup (if desired), and vanilla extract (if using).
3. **Add Ice:** Add the ice cubes if you're using fresh strawberries and want a colder, thicker smoothie.
4. **Blend Until Smooth:** Blend on high until the mixture is smooth and creamy. If it's too thick, you can add a bit more milk to achieve your preferred consistency.
5. **Taste and Adjust:** Taste the smoothie and adjust sweetness or add more milk if needed.
6. **Serve:** Pour into glasses and enjoy immediately!

For extra flavor, you can also add a handful of spinach for a green twist, or a tablespoon of chia seeds or flaxseeds for added nutrition.

Mango Pineapple Smoothie

Ingredients:

- 1 cup fresh or frozen mango chunks
- 1 cup fresh or frozen pineapple chunks
- 1 cup coconut water or fruit juice (like orange juice or apple juice)
- 1/2 cup Greek yogurt or coconut milk (for creaminess, optional)
- 1 tablespoon honey or maple syrup (optional, adjust to taste)
- 1/2 cup ice cubes (if using fresh fruit and you want a colder smoothie)

Instructions:

1. **Prepare the Fruit:** If using fresh mango and pineapple, peel and chop them into chunks.
2. **Blend:** In a blender, combine the mango chunks, pineapple chunks, coconut water (or juice), Greek yogurt (or coconut milk), and honey or maple syrup (if using).
3. **Add Ice:** Add the ice cubes if you're using fresh fruit and prefer a thicker, chilled smoothie.
4. **Blend Until Smooth:** Blend on high until the mixture is smooth and creamy. If the smoothie is too thick, add a little more coconut water or juice to reach your desired consistency.
5. **Taste and Adjust:** Taste the smoothie and adjust the sweetness or add more liquid if needed.
6. **Serve:** Pour into glasses and enjoy immediately!

For an extra tropical twist, you can also add a handful of spinach or kale for added nutrition, or a squeeze of lime juice for a zesty kick.

Blueberry Almond Smoothie

Ingredients:

- 1 cup fresh or frozen blueberries
- 1 banana (for natural sweetness and creaminess)
- 1 cup almond milk (or any milk of your choice)
- 1/4 cup almond butter or 2 tablespoons of almond meal (for a nutty flavor)
- 1/2 cup Greek yogurt (optional for extra creaminess)
- 1 tablespoon honey or maple syrup (optional, adjust to taste)
- 1/2 teaspoon vanilla extract (optional)
- 1/2 cup ice cubes (if using fresh blueberries and you want a colder smoothie)

Instructions:

1. **Prepare the Fruit:** If using fresh blueberries, wash them thoroughly. Peel and chop the banana into chunks.
2. **Blend:** In a blender, combine the blueberries, banana, almond milk, almond butter (or almond meal), Greek yogurt (if using), and honey or maple syrup (if desired).
3. **Add Ice:** Add the ice cubes if you're using fresh blueberries and want a thicker, cooler smoothie.
4. **Blend Until Smooth:** Blend on high until the mixture is smooth and creamy. If the smoothie is too thick, add a bit more almond milk to reach your desired consistency.
5. **Taste and Adjust:** Taste the smoothie and adjust the sweetness or add more almond milk if needed.
6. **Serve:** Pour into glasses and enjoy immediately!

For a boost of nutrition, you can add a handful of spinach or kale, or a tablespoon of chia seeds or flaxseeds.

Green Detox Smoothie

Ingredients:

- 1 cup spinach or kale (or a mix of both)
- 1 green apple, cored and chopped
- 1/2 cucumber, peeled and chopped
- 1/2 avocado (for creaminess)
- 1 banana (for natural sweetness)
- 1 cup coconut water or filtered water (or any liquid of your choice)
- 1 tablespoon lemon juice (for a zesty kick)
- 1 tablespoon chia seeds or flaxseeds (optional, for added fiber and omega-3s)
- 1/2 cup ice cubes (if you like it extra chilled)

Instructions:

1. **Prepare the Ingredients:** Wash the spinach or kale thoroughly. Core and chop the apple, peel and chop the cucumber, and slice the avocado.
2. **Blend:** In a blender, combine the spinach or kale, apple, cucumber, avocado, banana, coconut water (or filtered water), and lemon juice.
3. **Add Seeds and Ice:** Add chia seeds or flaxseeds if using, and the ice cubes if you want a colder, thicker smoothie.
4. **Blend Until Smooth:** Blend on high until the mixture is smooth and creamy. If the smoothie is too thick, add more liquid to reach your desired consistency.
5. **Taste and Adjust:** Taste the smoothie and adjust the sweetness or add more lemon juice if needed.
6. **Serve:** Pour into glasses and enjoy immediately!

Feel free to experiment with other green vegetables or fruits, like celery or kiwi, to personalize your smoothie.

Avocado Cilantro Lime Dressing

Ingredients:

- 1 ripe avocado
- 1/2 cup fresh cilantro leaves (packed)
- Juice of 1 lime
- 1/4 cup olive oil (or avocado oil)
- 1/4 cup water (or more as needed for consistency)
- 1 small garlic clove, minced
- 1/2 teaspoon ground cumin
- Salt and pepper to taste

Instructions:

1. **Prepare the Avocado:** Cut the avocado in half, remove the pit, and scoop the flesh into a blender or food processor.
2. **Add Ingredients:** Add the cilantro leaves, lime juice, olive oil, water, minced garlic, ground cumin, salt, and pepper.
3. **Blend:** Blend until the mixture is smooth and creamy. If the dressing is too thick, add a little more water until you reach your desired consistency.
4. **Taste and Adjust:** Taste the dressing and adjust the seasoning as needed. You can add more lime juice for extra tang or more salt for enhanced flavor.
5. **Serve or Store:** Transfer the dressing to a bowl or jar. It can be used immediately or stored in the refrigerator for up to 3-4 days. If it thickens in the fridge, you can thin it out with a little water or lime juice.

This dressing pairs wonderfully with a variety of dishes and adds a fresh, vibrant flavor!

Classic Hummus

Ingredients:

- 1 can (15 ounces) chickpeas (garbanzo beans), drained and rinsed
- 1/4 cup tahini (sesame seed paste)
- 1/4 cup fresh lemon juice (about 1 lemon)
- 1 small garlic clove, minced
- 2 tablespoons extra-virgin olive oil
- 1/2 teaspoon ground cumin
- Salt to taste (about 1/2 teaspoon)
- 2-3 tablespoons water (adjust for desired consistency)
- Optional: Paprika and additional olive oil for garnish

Instructions:

1. **Prepare the Chickpeas:** If you want a smoother texture, you can peel the chickpeas, though this step is optional. To peel, gently rub the chickpeas between your fingers to remove the skins.
2. **Blend Ingredients:** In a food processor or blender, combine the tahini and lemon juice. Blend for about 1 minute until smooth. This step helps to cream the tahini and give the hummus a smooth texture.
3. **Add Remaining Ingredients:** Add the minced garlic, olive oil, ground cumin, salt, and drained chickpeas. Blend until the mixture is smooth.
4. **Adjust Consistency:** If the hummus is too thick, add water a tablespoon at a time until you reach your desired consistency. Blend again to incorporate the water fully.
5. **Taste and Adjust:** Taste the hummus and adjust the seasoning if necessary. You might want to add more salt, lemon juice, or cumin depending on your preference.
6. **Serve:** Transfer the hummus to a serving bowl. Drizzle with a little extra olive oil and sprinkle with paprika if desired.
7. **Store:** Store any leftovers in an airtight container in the refrigerator for up to a week. Hummus can also be frozen for up to 3 months; just thaw and stir before serving.

Enjoy your homemade hummus with pita bread, vegetables, or as a spread for sandwiches!

Spicy Roasted Red Pepper Hummus

Ingredients:

- 1 can (15 ounces) chickpeas (garbanzo beans), drained and rinsed
- 1/2 cup roasted red peppers (jarred or homemade, well-drained)
- 1/4 cup tahini (sesame seed paste)
- 1/4 cup fresh lemon juice (about 1 lemon)
- 1-2 cloves garlic, minced
- 2 tablespoons extra-virgin olive oil
- 1/2 teaspoon ground cumin
- 1/4 teaspoon smoked paprika (optional, for extra smoky flavor)
- 1/4 to 1/2 teaspoon cayenne pepper (adjust to taste for spiciness)
- Salt to taste (about 1/2 teaspoon)
- 2-3 tablespoons water (adjust for desired consistency)
- Optional: Red pepper flakes and extra olive oil for garnish

Instructions:

1. **Prepare the Roasted Red Peppers:**
   - If using jarred roasted red peppers, drain them well. If using fresh, roast them (instructions below) and peel off the skins.
2. **Roasting Red Peppers (if using fresh):**
   - Preheat your oven to 450°F (230°C).
   - Place whole red peppers on a baking sheet and roast for 20-25 minutes, turning occasionally, until the skin is charred and blistered.
   - Remove from the oven and place in a bowl covered with plastic wrap for 10 minutes. This will help loosen the skin.
   - Peel off the charred skin, remove the stem and seeds, and chop the peppers.
3. **Blend Ingredients:**
   - In a food processor or high-speed blender, combine the tahini and lemon juice. Blend for about 1 minute until smooth. This helps to emulsify the tahini and lemon juice, creating a creamy base.
   - Add the roasted red peppers, minced garlic, olive oil, ground cumin, smoked paprika (if using), cayenne pepper, and salt. Blend until the mixture is smooth and well combined.
4. **Adjust Consistency:**
   - If the hummus is too thick, add water a tablespoon at a time until you reach your desired consistency. Blend again to incorporate the water fully.
5. **Taste and Adjust:**
   - Taste the hummus and adjust the seasoning as needed. You can add more cayenne pepper for extra heat or more lemon juice for tanginess.
6. **Serve:**

- Transfer the hummus to a serving bowl. Drizzle with a little extra olive oil and sprinkle with red pepper flakes if desired for extra spice and visual appeal.
7. **Store:**
    - Store any leftovers in an airtight container in the refrigerator for up to a week. Hummus can also be frozen for up to 3 months; thaw and stir before serving.

Enjoy this flavorful hummus as a dip with pita chips, fresh veggies, or as a spread for sandwiches and wraps!

Creamy Tomato Basil Soup

Ingredients:

- 2 tablespoons olive oil
- 1 large onion, chopped
- 3 cloves garlic, minced
- 1 (28-ounce) can crushed tomatoes (or about 4 cups of fresh tomatoes, peeled and chopped)
- 2 cups vegetable broth (or chicken broth)
- 1 teaspoon dried basil (or 1 tablespoon fresh basil, chopped)
- 1/2 teaspoon dried oregano
- 1/4 teaspoon red pepper flakes (optional, for a bit of heat)
- 1 cup heavy cream or half-and-half
- Salt and freshly ground black pepper to taste
- Fresh basil leaves for garnish (optional)

Instructions:

1. **Sauté the Aromatics:**
    - Heat the olive oil in a large pot over medium heat.
    - Add the chopped onion and cook until it becomes translucent, about 5-7 minutes.
    - Add the minced garlic and cook for another 1-2 minutes until fragrant, but be careful not to let it burn.
2. **Add Tomatoes and Broth:**
    - Stir in the crushed tomatoes, vegetable broth, dried basil, dried oregano, and red pepper flakes (if using).
    - Bring the mixture to a simmer and let it cook for about 15-20 minutes to let the flavors meld together.
3. **Blend the Soup:**
    - Use an immersion blender to blend the soup until smooth. Alternatively, you can carefully transfer the soup in batches to a regular blender. Be sure to let it cool slightly before blending and blend in batches to avoid splatters.
4. **Add Cream:**
    - Return the blended soup to the pot (if you used a regular blender).
    - Stir in the heavy cream or half-and-half and cook over low heat until the soup is heated through, about 5 minutes.
5. **Season and Serve:**
    - Taste the soup and adjust the seasoning with salt and pepper as needed.
    - Ladle the soup into bowls and garnish with fresh basil leaves if desired.
6. **Optional Garnishes:**
    - For extra flavor, you can garnish with a drizzle of olive oil, a sprinkle of Parmesan cheese, or croutons.

Enjoy this creamy tomato basil soup with a side of crusty bread or a grilled cheese sandwich for a classic comfort meal!

Butternut Squash Soup

Ingredients:

- 1 large butternut squash (about 3-4 pounds), peeled, seeded, and cubed
- 2 tablespoons olive oil
- 1 large onion, chopped
- 2 cloves garlic, minced
- 4 cups vegetable broth (or chicken broth)
- 1/2 teaspoon ground cumin
- 1/2 teaspoon ground ginger
- 1/4 teaspoon ground nutmeg
- 1/4 teaspoon ground cinnamon
- Salt and freshly ground black pepper to taste
- 1/2 cup heavy cream or coconut milk (optional for added creaminess)
- Fresh parsley or thyme for garnish (optional)

Instructions:

1. **Prepare the Butternut Squash:**
    - Preheat your oven to 400°F (200°C).
    - Peel the butternut squash, cut it in half, and scoop out the seeds. Then cut it into 1-inch cubes.
    - Toss the cubed squash with 1 tablespoon of olive oil and a pinch of salt and pepper. Spread the cubes in a single layer on a baking sheet.
2. **Roast the Squash:**
    - Roast in the preheated oven for 25-30 minutes, or until the squash is tender and caramelized, stirring halfway through.
3. **Sauté Aromatics:**
    - While the squash is roasting, heat the remaining 1 tablespoon of olive oil in a large pot over medium heat.
    - Add the chopped onion and cook until it becomes translucent, about 5-7 minutes.
    - Add the minced garlic and cook for another 1-2 minutes until fragrant.
4. **Combine and Cook:**
    - Add the roasted butternut squash to the pot with the onions and garlic.
    - Stir in the vegetable broth and spices (cumin, ginger, nutmeg, cinnamon). Bring the mixture to a simmer and cook for about 10 minutes, allowing the flavors to meld.
5. **Blend the Soup:**
    - Use an immersion blender to blend the soup until smooth. Alternatively, carefully transfer the soup in batches to a regular blender. Let it cool slightly before blending, and blend in batches to avoid splatters.
6. **Add Cream:**

- Return the blended soup to the pot (if you used a regular blender). Stir in the heavy cream or coconut milk if using, and cook over low heat until the soup is heated through.
7. **Season and Serve:**
    - Taste the soup and adjust the seasoning with salt and pepper as needed.
    - Ladle the soup into bowls and garnish with fresh parsley or thyme if desired.
8. **Optional Garnishes:**
    - You can also garnish with a drizzle of olive oil, a dollop of yogurt or sour cream, or a sprinkle of roasted pumpkin seeds for added texture.

Enjoy this rich and velvety butternut squash soup with a slice of crusty bread or a simple salad!

Spicy Carrot Soup

Ingredients:

- 2 tablespoons olive oil
- 1 large onion, chopped
- 3 cloves garlic, minced
- 1-inch piece of fresh ginger, peeled and minced
- 1 pound carrots, peeled and chopped (about 4-5 medium carrots)
- 1 medium potato, peeled and chopped (for creaminess, optional)
- 1 teaspoon ground cumin
- 1/2 teaspoon ground coriander
- 1/4 to 1/2 teaspoon cayenne pepper (adjust to taste for spiciness)
- 1/2 teaspoon smoked paprika (optional, for extra smoky flavor)
- 4 cups vegetable broth (or chicken broth)
- Salt and freshly ground black pepper to taste
- 1/2 cup coconut milk or heavy cream (optional, for added creaminess)
- Fresh cilantro or parsley for garnish (optional)

Instructions:

1. **Sauté Aromatics:**
   - Heat the olive oil in a large pot over medium heat.
   - Add the chopped onion and cook until translucent, about 5-7 minutes.
   - Add the minced garlic and ginger and cook for another 1-2 minutes until fragrant.
2. **Add Carrots and Spices:**
   - Add the chopped carrots (and potato if using) to the pot.
   - Stir in the ground cumin, ground coriander, cayenne pepper, and smoked paprika (if using). Cook for 1-2 minutes, allowing the spices to become fragrant.
3. **Add Broth and Simmer:**
   - Pour in the vegetable broth and bring the mixture to a boil.
   - Reduce the heat to low and simmer for about 20-25 minutes, or until the carrots (and potato) are tender.
4. **Blend the Soup:**
   - Use an immersion blender to blend the soup until smooth. Alternatively, carefully transfer the soup in batches to a regular blender. Let it cool slightly before blending, and blend in batches to avoid splatters.
5. **Add Creaminess:**
   - Return the blended soup to the pot (if you used a regular blender). Stir in the coconut milk or heavy cream if using, and cook over low heat until the soup is heated through.
6. **Season and Serve:**
   - Taste the soup and adjust the seasoning with salt and pepper as needed. Add more cayenne pepper if you prefer additional heat.

- Ladle the soup into bowls and garnish with fresh cilantro or parsley if desired.
7. **Optional Garnishes:**
    - For added texture and flavor, consider garnishing with a swirl of yogurt or sour cream, a sprinkle of chili flakes, or a drizzle of olive oil.

This spicy carrot soup pairs wonderfully with crusty bread or a simple salad for a satisfying meal. Enjoy the warming, vibrant flavors!

Vegan Creamy Mushroom Soup

Ingredients:

- 2 tablespoons olive oil
- 1 large onion, chopped
- 3 cloves garlic, minced
- 1 pound mushrooms (button, cremini, or a mix), sliced
- 1 large carrot, peeled and chopped
- 1 celery stalk, chopped
- 1 teaspoon dried thyme (or 1 tablespoon fresh thyme, chopped)
- 1/2 teaspoon dried rosemary (optional)
- 4 cups vegetable broth
- 1 cup full-fat coconut milk (or unsweetened almond milk for a lighter option)
- 2 tablespoons nutritional yeast (for a cheesy flavor, optional)
- 1 tablespoon all-purpose flour or cornstarch (optional, for thickening)
- Salt and freshly ground black pepper to taste
- Fresh parsley or thyme for garnish (optional)

Instructions:

1. **Sauté the Aromatics:**
   - Heat the olive oil in a large pot over medium heat.
   - Add the chopped onion and cook until it becomes translucent, about 5-7 minutes.
   - Add the minced garlic and cook for another 1-2 minutes until fragrant.
2. **Cook the Vegetables:**
   - Add the sliced mushrooms, chopped carrot, and celery to the pot. Cook, stirring occasionally, until the mushrooms release their moisture and become browned, about 10 minutes.
3. **Add Spices and Broth:**
   - Stir in the dried thyme and rosemary (if using).
   - Pour in the vegetable broth and bring the mixture to a boil.
   - Reduce the heat to low and simmer for about 15-20 minutes, or until the carrots are tender.
4. **Blend the Soup:**
   - Use an immersion blender to blend the soup until smooth. Alternatively, carefully transfer the soup in batches to a regular blender. Let it cool slightly before blending, and blend in batches to avoid splatters.
5. **Add Creaminess:**
   - Return the blended soup to the pot (if you used a regular blender).
   - Stir in the coconut milk and nutritional yeast (if using). Cook over low heat until the soup is heated through.
6. **Thicken the Soup (optional):**

- If you prefer a thicker soup, mix the flour or cornstarch with a bit of cold water to make a slurry. Stir it into the soup and cook for an additional 5 minutes, until the soup thickens.
7. **Season and Serve:**
   - Taste the soup and adjust the seasoning with salt and pepper as needed.
   - Ladle the soup into bowls and garnish with fresh parsley or thyme if desired.
8. **Optional Garnishes:**
   - Consider adding a swirl of extra coconut milk, sautéed mushrooms, or a sprinkle of fresh herbs for added texture and flavor.

This vegan creamy mushroom soup is perfect as a hearty starter or a light main course. Enjoy it with crusty bread or a simple salad!

Chocolate Peanut Butter Milkshake

Ingredients:

- 2 cups vanilla ice cream
- 1/2 cup milk (dairy or non-dairy, such as almond, soy, or oat milk)
- 1/4 cup creamy peanut butter
- 1/4 cup chocolate syrup (or 2 tablespoons unsweetened cocoa powder plus 2 tablespoons honey or maple syrup)
- 1/2 teaspoon vanilla extract (optional)
- Whipped cream (optional, for topping)
- Extra chocolate syrup or peanut butter (optional, for drizzling)

Instructions:

1. **Blend Ingredients:**
    - In a blender, combine the vanilla ice cream, milk, creamy peanut butter, chocolate syrup, and vanilla extract (if using).
    - Blend on high until smooth and creamy. If the milkshake is too thick, add a bit more milk to reach your desired consistency. If it's too thin, add a bit more ice cream.
2. **Serve:**
    - Pour the milkshake into glasses.
3. **Optional Toppings:**
    - Top with whipped cream if desired.
    - Drizzle extra chocolate syrup or peanut butter over the whipped cream for added indulgence.
    - You can also garnish with chocolate shavings or crushed peanuts for extra texture.
4. **Enjoy:**
    - Serve immediately with a straw and enjoy your creamy, delicious milkshake!

Feel free to customize this recipe by adding mix-ins like crushed cookies or a handful of chocolate chips before blending, or by using different flavored ice creams.

Vanilla Almond Protein Shake

Ingredients:

- 1 scoop vanilla protein powder (whey or plant-based)
- 1 cup unsweetened almond milk (or any milk of your choice)
- 1/4 cup almond butter or 2 tablespoons almond meal
- 1/2 teaspoon vanilla extract
- 1/2 banana (for natural sweetness and creaminess)
- 1 tablespoon chia seeds or flaxseeds (optional, for added fiber and omega-3s)
- 1/2 cup ice cubes (if you want a thicker, colder shake)
- Sweetener to taste (like honey or maple syrup, optional)

Instructions:

1. **Combine Ingredients:**
   - In a blender, add the vanilla protein powder, almond milk, almond butter (or almond meal), vanilla extract, and banana.
2. **Add Optional Ingredients:**
   - If using, add the chia seeds or flaxseeds for added nutrition.
   - Add ice cubes if you prefer a thicker, colder shake.
3. **Blend:**
   - Blend on high until smooth and creamy. If the shake is too thick, add a bit more almond milk until you reach your desired consistency.
4. **Taste and Adjust:**
   - Taste the shake and add sweetener if needed, blending again to combine.
5. **Serve:**
   - Pour into a glass and enjoy immediately.

Feel free to customize your shake by adding other ingredients like a handful of spinach for a green boost, a spoonful of cocoa powder for a chocolate twist, or a few berries for added flavor.

Berry Oatmeal Smoothie

Ingredients:

- 1/2 cup rolled oats
- 1 cup mixed berries (fresh or frozen; such as strawberries, blueberries, raspberries, or blackberries)
- 1/2 banana (for natural sweetness and creaminess)
- 1 cup almond milk (or any milk of your choice)
- 1 tablespoon honey or maple syrup (optional, for added sweetness)
- 1/2 teaspoon vanilla extract (optional, for extra flavor)
- 1 tablespoon chia seeds or flaxseeds (optional, for added fiber and omega-3s)
- 1/2 cup Greek yogurt or a dairy-free yogurt alternative (optional, for extra creaminess and protein)
- 1/2 cup ice cubes (if using fresh berries or for a thicker smoothie)

Instructions:

1. **Prepare the Oats:**
   - If you have time, soak the rolled oats in a small bowl with a little bit of water or milk for about 10 minutes. This helps them blend more smoothly. If you're short on time, you can skip this step.
2. **Blend Ingredients:**
   - In a blender, combine the rolled oats, mixed berries, banana, almond milk, honey or maple syrup (if using), and vanilla extract (if using).
   - Add the chia seeds or flaxseeds and Greek yogurt (if using).
3. **Blend:**
   - Blend on high until smooth and creamy. If the smoothie is too thick, add a bit more almond milk to reach your desired consistency. If it's too thin, add a few more oats or some more frozen berries.
4. **Add Ice (if desired):**
   - If you like your smoothie colder and thicker, add ice cubes and blend again until well combined.
5. **Taste and Adjust:**
   - Taste the smoothie and adjust sweetness or thickness as needed. Add more honey or syrup for extra sweetness or more berries for a fruitier flavor.
6. **Serve:**
   - Pour into a glass and enjoy immediately.

This Berry Oatmeal Smoothie is perfect for breakfast on the go, a post-workout snack, or a refreshing afternoon treat.

Pineapple Coconut Smoothie

Ingredients:

- 1 cup fresh or frozen pineapple chunks
- 1/2 cup coconut milk (full-fat or light, depending on your preference)
- 1/2 cup Greek yogurt or coconut yogurt (for extra creaminess; optional)
- 1 banana (for added creaminess and natural sweetness)
- 1 tablespoon shredded coconut (optional, for extra coconut flavor and texture)
- 1 tablespoon honey or maple syrup (optional, for added sweetness)
- 1/2 cup ice cubes (if using fresh pineapple or for a thicker smoothie)

Instructions:

1. **Prepare Ingredients:**
    - If using fresh pineapple, you can cut it into chunks. If using frozen pineapple, there's no need to thaw it beforehand.
2. **Blend Ingredients:**
    - In a blender, combine the pineapple chunks, coconut milk, Greek yogurt (if using), banana, and shredded coconut (if using).
    - Add honey or maple syrup if you prefer a sweeter smoothie.
3. **Blend:**
    - Blend on high until smooth and creamy. If the smoothie is too thick, add a bit more coconut milk to reach your desired consistency. If it's too thin, add a few more pineapple chunks or ice cubes.
4. **Add Ice (if desired):**
    - If you prefer a thicker and colder smoothie, add ice cubes and blend again until well combined.
5. **Taste and Adjust:**
    - Taste the smoothie and adjust the sweetness or coconut flavor as needed. Add more honey or shredded coconut if desired.
6. **Serve:**
    - Pour into a glass and enjoy immediately. Garnish with a sprinkle of shredded coconut or a pineapple slice for an extra touch of tropical flair.

This Pineapple Coconut Smoothie is perfect for a refreshing breakfast, a post-workout treat, or a tropical escape any time of day.

Kale Pineapple Smoothie

Ingredients:

- 1 cup fresh kale leaves (stems removed)
- 1 cup fresh or frozen pineapple chunks
- 1/2 banana (for added creaminess and natural sweetness)
- 1/2 cup Greek yogurt or non-dairy yogurt (for extra creaminess; optional)
- 1/2 cup coconut water or almond milk (or any milk of your choice)
- 1 tablespoon chia seeds or flaxseeds (optional, for added fiber and omega-3s)
- 1 tablespoon honey or maple syrup (optional, for added sweetness)
- 1/2 cup ice cubes (if using fresh pineapple or for a thicker smoothie)

Instructions:

1. **Prepare Ingredients:**
   - Remove the stems from the kale leaves and roughly chop them. If using fresh pineapple, cut it into chunks. If using frozen pineapple, there's no need to thaw it beforehand.
2. **Blend Ingredients:**
   - In a blender, combine the kale leaves, pineapple chunks, banana, Greek yogurt (if using), and coconut water or almond milk.
   - Add chia seeds or flaxseeds if desired.
3. **Blend:**
   - Blend on high until smooth and creamy. If the smoothie is too thick, add more coconut water or almond milk to reach your desired consistency. If it's too thin, add a few more pineapple chunks or ice cubes.
4. **Add Ice (if desired):**
   - If you prefer a thicker and colder smoothie, add ice cubes and blend again until well combined.
5. **Taste and Adjust:**
   - Taste the smoothie and adjust the sweetness if needed. Add honey or maple syrup if you prefer a sweeter smoothie.
6. **Serve:**
   - Pour into a glass and enjoy immediately. You can garnish with a few pineapple chunks or a sprinkle of chia seeds for added texture.

This Kale Pineapple Smoothie is a great way to incorporate more greens into your diet while still enjoying a refreshing and flavorful drink.

Apple Cinnamon Smoothie

Ingredients:

- 1 large apple, cored and chopped (leave the skin on for added fiber and nutrients)
- 1/2 banana (for creaminess and natural sweetness)
- 1/2 cup Greek yogurt or non-dairy yogurt (for extra creaminess; optional)
- 1 cup almond milk or any milk of your choice
- 1/2 teaspoon ground cinnamon (adjust to taste)
- 1/4 teaspoon vanilla extract (optional, for extra flavor)
- 1 tablespoon honey or maple syrup (optional, for added sweetness)
- 1/4 cup rolled oats (optional, for added fiber and texture)
- 1/2 cup ice cubes (if using fresh apple or for a thicker smoothie)

Instructions:

1. **Prepare Ingredients:**
   - Core and chop the apple into chunks. You can leave the skin on for added nutrients, but peel it if you prefer a smoother texture.
   - If you're using rolled oats, consider soaking them in a bit of milk for 5 minutes to make them easier to blend.
2. **Blend:**
   - In a blender, combine the chopped apple, banana, Greek yogurt (if using), almond milk, ground cinnamon, and vanilla extract (if using).
   - Add honey or maple syrup if you want a sweeter smoothie.
   - If using, add the soaked rolled oats.
3. **Blend Until Smooth:**
   - Blend on high until the mixture is smooth and creamy. If the smoothie is too thick, add more milk to reach your desired consistency. If it's too thin, add a few more apple chunks or some ice cubes.
4. **Add Ice (if desired):**
   - For a colder and thicker smoothie, add ice cubes and blend again until well combined.
5. **Taste and Adjust:**
   - Taste the smoothie and adjust the sweetness or cinnamon to your liking. Add more honey or syrup if needed, or a pinch more cinnamon for extra flavor.
6. **Serve:**
   - Pour the smoothie into a glass and enjoy immediately. For an extra touch, garnish with a sprinkle of cinnamon or a few apple slices.

This Apple Cinnamon Smoothie is a tasty and healthy way to enjoy classic fall flavors any time of the year.

Sweet Potato Pie Smoothie

Ingredients:

- 1 cup cooked and mashed sweet potato (about 1 medium sweet potato)
- 1/2 banana (for natural sweetness and creaminess)
- 1/2 cup Greek yogurt or non-dairy yogurt (for extra creaminess; optional)
- 1 cup almond milk or any milk of your choice
- 1/2 teaspoon ground cinnamon
- 1/4 teaspoon ground nutmeg
- 1/4 teaspoon ground ginger
- 1 tablespoon maple syrup or honey (optional, for added sweetness)
- 1/4 cup rolled oats (optional, for added fiber and texture)
- 1/2 cup ice cubes (if using fresh sweet potato or for a thicker smoothie)

Instructions:

1. **Prepare Sweet Potato:**
    - Cook and mash the sweet potato. You can bake or steam it until tender, then mash it with a fork or blend until smooth. If you're using leftover sweet potato pie filling, it will work too, but adjust the spices and sweetness accordingly.
2. **Blend Ingredients:**
    - In a blender, combine the mashed sweet potato, banana, Greek yogurt (if using), almond milk, ground cinnamon, nutmeg, ginger, and maple syrup or honey.
    - If using, add the rolled oats.
3. **Blend Until Smooth:**
    - Blend on high until smooth and creamy. If the smoothie is too thick, add more almond milk to reach your desired consistency. If it's too thin, add a bit more mashed sweet potato or ice cubes.
4. **Add Ice (if desired):**
    - For a colder and thicker smoothie, add ice cubes and blend again until well combined.
5. **Taste and Adjust:**
    - Taste the smoothie and adjust the spices or sweetness to your liking. Add more maple syrup or honey if needed, or a pinch more cinnamon and nutmeg for extra flavor.
6. **Serve:**
    - Pour the smoothie into a glass and enjoy immediately. Garnish with a sprinkle of cinnamon or a dollop of whipped cream for an extra treat.

This Sweet Potato Pie Smoothie offers a rich, creamy texture and comforting spice blend that captures the essence of sweet potato pie in a healthy, refreshing way.

Greek Yogurt Pancake Batter

Ingredients:

- 1 cup all-purpose flour
- 1 tablespoon sugar (optional, adjust to taste)
- 1 tablespoon baking powder
- 1/4 teaspoon salt
- 1 cup Greek yogurt (plain or vanilla)
- 1/2 cup milk (dairy or non-dairy, such as almond or oat milk)
- 1 large egg
- 2 tablespoons melted butter or vegetable oil
- 1 teaspoon vanilla extract (optional, for added flavor)

Instructions:

1. **Mix Dry Ingredients:**
   - In a large bowl, whisk together the flour, sugar (if using), baking powder, and salt.
2. **Combine Wet Ingredients:**
   - In a separate bowl, mix the Greek yogurt, milk, egg, melted butter or oil, and vanilla extract (if using).
3. **Combine Wet and Dry Ingredients:**
   - Pour the wet ingredients into the dry ingredients.
   - Gently fold the ingredients together until just combined. Be careful not to overmix; a few lumps are okay. Overmixing can lead to dense pancakes.
4. **Cook the Pancakes:**
   - Heat a non-stick skillet or griddle over medium heat and lightly grease it with butter or oil.
   - Pour 1/4 cup of batter onto the skillet for each pancake.
   - Cook until bubbles form on the surface and the edges start to look set, about 2-3 minutes. Flip and cook for another 1-2 minutes, or until golden brown and cooked through.
5. **Serve:**
   - Serve the pancakes warm with your favorite toppings, such as fresh fruit, maple syrup, yogurt, or a sprinkle of powdered sugar.

Tips:

- For extra flavor, you can add mix-ins like blueberries, chocolate chips, or nuts to the batter before cooking.
- If you prefer a thinner batter, add a bit more milk until you reach the desired consistency.
- For fluffier pancakes, let the batter rest for about 5 minutes before cooking.

These Greek Yogurt Pancakes are fluffy and delicious, with a slight tang from the yogurt and a protein boost that makes them even more satisfying. Enjoy your pancakes with your favorite toppings for a perfect breakfast or brunch!

Easy Blender Salsa

Ingredients:

- 1 can (14.5 oz) diced tomatoes (or 2 cups fresh tomatoes, chopped)
- 1/2 onion, roughly chopped
- 1-2 cloves garlic, peeled
- 1 jalapeño or serrano pepper (seeds removed for less heat, or keep some seeds for extra spiciness)
- 1/4 cup fresh cilantro leaves (stems removed)
- Juice of 1 lime
- 1/2 teaspoon ground cumin
- Salt and pepper to taste

Instructions:

1. **Prepare Ingredients:**
   - If using fresh tomatoes, chop them roughly. If using canned tomatoes, drain them slightly to avoid excess liquid.
2. **Blend:**
   - In a blender, combine the tomatoes, chopped onion, garlic cloves, jalapeño (or serrano pepper), cilantro, lime juice, and ground cumin.
   - Blend on high until the salsa reaches your desired consistency. For a chunkier salsa, blend for a shorter time. For a smoother salsa, blend longer.
3. **Season:**
   - Taste the salsa and add salt and pepper to your liking. You can also adjust the heat by adding more jalapeño or serrano pepper if desired.
4. **Chill (Optional):**
   - For the best flavor, let the salsa sit in the refrigerator for at least 30 minutes to allow the flavors to meld together.
5. **Serve:**
   - Serve with tortilla chips, as a topping for tacos or grilled meats, or as a fresh condiment for your favorite dishes.

Tips:

- If you prefer a smokier flavor, you can roast the tomatoes, onion, and garlic before blending.
- For a bit of sweetness, add a small amount of sugar or a chopped red bell pepper.
- If the salsa is too thick, add a little water or extra lime juice to reach your desired consistency.

This Easy Blender Salsa is fresh, flavorful, and perfect for any occasion, from casual snacking to party appetizers. Enjoy!

Roasted Tomato Sauce

Ingredients:

- 2 pounds ripe tomatoes (such as Roma or vine-ripened)
- 1/4 cup olive oil
- 1 large onion, chopped
- 4 cloves garlic, minced
- 1 teaspoon dried oregano
- 1 teaspoon dried basil
- 1/2 teaspoon sugar (optional, to balance acidity)
- Salt and freshly ground black pepper to taste
- 1/4 cup fresh basil leaves, chopped (optional, for extra flavor)
- 1 tablespoon balsamic vinegar (optional, for added depth)

Instructions:

1. **Prepare the Tomatoes:**
   - Preheat your oven to 400°F (200°C).
   - Wash and core the tomatoes. Cut them into halves or quarters, depending on their size.
2. **Roast the Tomatoes:**
   - Place the tomatoes on a baking sheet, cut side up. Drizzle with olive oil and season with salt and pepper.
   - Roast in the preheated oven for about 25-30 minutes, or until the tomatoes are soft and slightly caramelized.
3. **Cook the Aromatics:**
   - While the tomatoes are roasting, heat a tablespoon of olive oil in a large saucepan over medium heat.
   - Add the chopped onion and cook until translucent and softened, about 5-7 minutes.
   - Add the minced garlic and cook for an additional 1-2 minutes until fragrant.
4. **Blend the Sauce:**
   - Once the tomatoes are roasted, remove them from the oven and let them cool slightly.
   - Transfer the roasted tomatoes, including any juices from the baking sheet, to a blender or food processor. Blend until smooth. Alternatively, you can use an immersion blender directly in the pot.
5. **Combine and Simmer:**
   - Add the blended tomatoes to the saucepan with the cooked onions and garlic.
   - Stir in the dried oregano, dried basil, and sugar (if using). Simmer the sauce over medium-low heat for about 15-20 minutes, allowing the flavors to meld together. If you prefer a thicker sauce, simmer for a longer time.
6. **Adjust Seasoning:**

- Taste the sauce and adjust the seasoning with additional salt, pepper, and fresh basil (if using).
- Stir in balsamic vinegar if desired for extra depth of flavor.
7. **Serve:**
   - Use the roasted tomato sauce immediately over pasta, pizza, or as a base for other dishes. It can also be cooled and stored in the refrigerator for up to a week or frozen for up to 3 months.

This Roasted Tomato Sauce is a versatile and flavorful addition to many dishes, perfect for adding a touch of homemade goodness to your meals.

Cashew Cheese Sauce

Ingredients:

- 1 cup raw cashews, soaked for at least 2 hours (or overnight)
- 1/2 cup water (or more as needed for desired consistency)
- 1/4 cup nutritional yeast (for a cheesy flavor)
- 1 tablespoon lemon juice (for tanginess)
- 1 teaspoon apple cider vinegar (optional, for extra tang)
- 1 garlic clove
- 1/2 teaspoon turmeric (for color, optional)
- 1/2 teaspoon smoked paprika (for a smoky flavor, optional)
- 1/2 teaspoon salt (or to taste)
- Freshly ground black pepper (to taste)

Instructions:

1. **Soak Cashews:**
   - If you haven't already, soak the cashews in water for at least 2 hours or overnight. This softens them and helps create a smooth sauce. If you're short on time, you can use hot water and soak for 20-30 minutes.
2. **Drain and Rinse:**
   - Drain and rinse the cashews thoroughly.
3. **Blend Ingredients:**
   - In a high-speed blender or food processor, combine the soaked cashews, water, nutritional yeast, lemon juice, apple cider vinegar (if using), garlic clove, turmeric (if using), smoked paprika (if using), salt, and black pepper.
4. **Blend Until Smooth:**
   - Blend on high until the mixture is completely smooth and creamy. You may need to stop and scrape down the sides or add a little more water if the sauce is too thick.
5. **Adjust Consistency and Flavor:**
   - Taste the sauce and adjust the seasoning if needed. For a thinner sauce, add more water, a tablespoon at a time, and blend until you reach your desired consistency.
6. **Heat (Optional):**
   - If you prefer a warm sauce, transfer it to a saucepan and heat over low heat, stirring occasionally until warmed through. Avoid boiling, as this can alter the texture.
7. **Serve:**
   - Use the cashew cheese sauce over pasta, roasted vegetables, nachos, or as a dip. It's a versatile sauce that can be used in a variety of dishes.

Tips:

- For a spicier version, add a pinch of cayenne pepper or a few dashes of hot sauce.
- If you don't have nutritional yeast, you can omit it, but it adds a distinctive cheesy flavor that enhances the sauce.

This Cashew Cheese Sauce is a creamy, dairy-free alternative that can be enjoyed by everyone, whether you're vegan, lactose-intolerant, or just looking for a healthier cheese sauce option.

Classic Guacamole

Ingredients:

- 3 ripe avocados
- 1 small onion, finely chopped
- 1-2 cloves garlic, minced
- 1-2 tomatoes, seeded and diced
- 1 jalapeño or serrano pepper, seeded and finely chopped (optional, for heat)
- Juice of 1 lime (adjust to taste)
- Salt to taste
- Freshly ground black pepper to taste
- 1/4 cup fresh cilantro, chopped (optional)

Instructions:

1. **Prepare the Avocados:**
   - Cut the avocados in half, remove the pits, and scoop the flesh into a mixing bowl.
   - Use a fork to mash the avocados to your desired consistency. Some people like it smooth, while others prefer it chunky.
2. **Mix in Vegetables:**
   - Add the finely chopped onion, minced garlic, diced tomatoes, and chopped jalapeño (if using) to the mashed avocado.
3. **Season:**
   - Add the lime juice, salt, and freshly ground black pepper. Mix everything together gently.
4. **Add Cilantro (Optional):**
   - Stir in the chopped cilantro if you're using it.
5. **Taste and Adjust:**
   - Taste the guacamole and adjust the seasoning as needed. You may want to add more lime juice, salt, or pepper depending on your preference.
6. **Serve:**
   - Serve the guacamole immediately with tortilla chips, or as a topping for tacos, burritos, or grilled meats.

Tips:

- To prevent the guacamole from browning, place a piece of plastic wrap directly on the surface of the guacamole before refrigerating. It can help to squeeze a bit of extra lime juice on top as well.
- If you prefer a spicier guacamole, leave some of the seeds from the jalapeño in the mix, or add a bit of hot sauce.

Enjoy your classic guacamole with friends and family for a fresh, flavorful, and always crowd-pleasing dip!

Cilantro Lime Rice

Ingredients:

- 1 cup long-grain white rice (such as Basmati or Jasmine)
- 2 cups water or chicken broth (for extra flavor)
- 1 tablespoon olive oil or butter
- 1/2 teaspoon salt
- Juice of 1 lime (or to taste)
- 1/4 cup fresh cilantro, chopped
- 1 garlic clove, minced (optional)
- 1/4 teaspoon ground cumin (optional, for extra flavor)

Instructions:

1. **Cook the Rice:**
   - Rinse the rice under cold water until the water runs clear. This helps remove excess starch and keeps the rice from becoming too sticky.
   - In a medium saucepan, heat the olive oil or butter over medium heat.
   - Add the rice and cook, stirring frequently, until the rice is lightly toasted and fragrant, about 2-3 minutes.
   - Add the water or chicken broth and salt. Bring to a boil.
2. **Simmer:**
   - Once boiling, reduce the heat to low, cover, and simmer for 15-18 minutes, or until the rice is tender and the liquid is absorbed. Avoid lifting the lid during cooking.
3. **Fluff and Season:**
   - Remove the saucepan from the heat and let it sit, covered, for 5 minutes.
   - Fluff the rice with a fork.
4. **Add Flavor:**
   - Stir in the lime juice, chopped cilantro, and minced garlic (if using).
   - If desired, add ground cumin for extra flavor. Adjust the seasoning with more salt or lime juice as needed.
5. **Serve:**
   - Serve the Cilantro Lime Rice warm as a side dish with your favorite Mexican or Tex-Mex meals, such as tacos, burritos, or grilled meats.

Tips:

- For added flavor, you can sauté the garlic in the oil before adding the rice, then proceed with toasting the rice.
- If you prefer a stronger lime flavor, you can add more lime juice or zest.

Cilantro Lime Rice is a versatile and delicious side that brings a burst of freshness to any meal. Enjoy!

Vegan Alfredo Sauce

Ingredients:

- 1 cup raw cashews, soaked for at least 2 hours (or use hot water for 20-30 minutes)
- 1 1/2 cups unsweetened almond milk (or any plant-based milk)
- 1/4 cup nutritional yeast (for a cheesy flavor)
- 2 tablespoons olive oil
- 1 tablespoon lemon juice
- 2 cloves garlic
- 1/2 teaspoon onion powder (optional)
- 1/4 teaspoon ground nutmeg (optional)
- Salt and freshly ground black pepper to taste

Instructions:

1. **Soak the Cashews:**
   - If you haven't already, soak the cashews in water for at least 2 hours, or use hot water for 20-30 minutes. Drain and rinse well.
2. **Blend Ingredients:**
   - In a high-speed blender, combine the soaked cashews, almond milk, nutritional yeast, olive oil, lemon juice, garlic, onion powder (if using), and ground nutmeg (if using).
   - Blend until completely smooth and creamy. This may take a few minutes, depending on your blender. If the sauce is too thick, add a bit more almond milk until you reach your desired consistency.
3. **Cook the Sauce:**
   - Pour the blended mixture into a saucepan over medium heat.
   - Cook, stirring frequently, until the sauce is heated through and has thickened slightly, about 5-7 minutes. Be careful not to let it boil.
4. **Season:**
   - Taste the sauce and adjust the seasoning with salt and black pepper to your liking.
5. **Serve:**
   - Toss the sauce with cooked pasta, or use it as a creamy topping for vegetables or grains.

Tips:

- For extra flavor, you can add a pinch of smoked paprika or a splash of white wine vinegar.
- To thicken the sauce, let it simmer for a few extra minutes. To thin it, add a bit more plant-based milk.
- If you prefer a more savory sauce, add a tablespoon of miso paste or a bit of soy sauce.

This Vegan Alfredo Sauce is a versatile and delicious option that can be enjoyed with your favorite pasta or used in a variety of dishes.

Smoothie Bowl Base

Ingredients:

- 1 cup frozen fruit (such as berries, mango, banana, or a combination)
- 1/2 banana (fresh or frozen, for creaminess)
- 1/2 cup Greek yogurt or non-dairy yogurt (for added creaminess; optional)
- 1/2 cup plant-based milk or any milk of your choice (adjust as needed)
- 1 tablespoon honey or maple syrup (optional, for added sweetness)
- 1 tablespoon chia seeds or flaxseeds (optional, for added nutrition)

Instructions:

1. **Prepare Ingredients:**
   - If using fresh fruit, consider freezing it beforehand to achieve a thicker, creamier texture.
2. **Blend:**
   - In a blender, combine the frozen fruit, banana, Greek yogurt (if using), and plant-based milk.
   - Blend until smooth and creamy. You might need to stop and scrape down the sides or add a bit more milk if the mixture is too thick.
3. **Adjust Consistency:**
   - If the base is too thick, add a bit more milk until you reach your desired consistency. If it's too thin, add more frozen fruit or a handful of ice cubes and blend again.
4. **Sweeten (Optional):**
   - Taste the base and add honey or maple syrup if you prefer a sweeter smoothie bowl.
5. **Add Seeds (Optional):**
   - If using chia seeds or flaxseeds, blend them in with the other ingredients, or stir them in after blending for added texture and nutrition.
6. **Serve:**
   - Pour the smoothie bowl base into a bowl and top with your favorite toppings.

Topping Ideas:

- Fresh fruit (sliced bananas, berries, kiwi, mango)
- Granola
- Nuts and seeds (almonds, chia seeds, flaxseeds)
- Coconut flakes
- Nut butters (almond, peanut, or cashew butter)
- A drizzle of honey or maple syrup

Tips:

- For an extra thick smoothie bowl, use less liquid and more frozen fruit.
- You can customize the flavor by adding a handful of spinach or kale for a green smoothie bowl, or a tablespoon of cocoa powder for a chocolate version.

This smoothie bowl base is a great starting point for a customizable, nutritious breakfast or snack, allowing you to create endless variations based on your preferences and what you have on hand. Enjoy experimenting with different toppings and flavors!

Vegan Creamy Caesar Dressing

Ingredients:

- 1/2 cup raw cashews, soaked for at least 2 hours or overnight (or use hot water for 20-30 minutes)
- 1/4 cup water (or more as needed for consistency)
- 1/4 cup nutritional yeast (for a cheesy flavor)
- 2 tablespoons lemon juice (about 1 lemon)
- 2 tablespoons Dijon mustard
- 2 cloves garlic
- 1 tablespoon capers (drained) or 1 tablespoon white miso paste (for a briny flavor)
- 1 tablespoon olive oil
- 1/4 teaspoon ground black pepper
- 1/2 teaspoon salt (or to taste)
- 1/4 teaspoon smoked paprika (optional, for a smoky flavor)

Instructions:

1. **Soak the Cashews:**
   - If you haven't already, soak the cashews in water for at least 2 hours or use hot water for 20-30 minutes. Drain and rinse well.
2. **Blend the Ingredients:**
   - In a high-speed blender or food processor, combine the soaked cashews, water, nutritional yeast, lemon juice, Dijon mustard, garlic, capers (or miso paste), olive oil, black pepper, and salt.
   - Blend until completely smooth and creamy. You may need to stop and scrape down the sides or add more water to achieve the desired consistency.
3. **Adjust Seasoning:**
   - Taste the dressing and adjust the seasoning with additional salt, pepper, or lemon juice as needed. If you like a stronger flavor, you can add a bit more capers or miso paste.
4. **Chill (Optional):**
   - For the best flavor, chill the dressing in the refrigerator for at least 30 minutes before using to allow the flavors to meld together.
5. **Serve:**
   - Use the Vegan Creamy Caesar Dressing on salads, as a dip for veggies, or as a spread for sandwiches.

Tips:

- If you prefer a thinner dressing, add a bit more water until you reach your desired consistency.

- For added tang, you can also incorporate a splash of apple cider vinegar or a teaspoon of vegan Worcestershire sauce.

This Vegan Creamy Caesar Dressing is a tasty, versatile option that provides all the richness of classic Caesar dressing while keeping it plant-based. Enjoy!

Healthy Strawberry Shortcake Smoothie

Ingredients:

- 1 cup frozen strawberries
- 1/2 cup Greek yogurt or non-dairy yogurt (for creaminess and protein)
- 1/2 banana (for natural sweetness and creaminess)
- 1/2 cup unsweetened almond milk (or any milk of your choice)
- 1 tablespoon almond butter or cashew butter (for a nutty flavor)
- 1 teaspoon vanilla extract
- 1/4 teaspoon ground cinnamon (optional, for extra flavor)
- 1 tablespoon honey or maple syrup (optional, for additional sweetness)
- 1/4 cup rolled oats (optional, for added fiber and texture)

Instructions:

1. **Blend Ingredients:**
   - In a blender, combine the frozen strawberries, Greek yogurt, banana, almond milk, almond butter, vanilla extract, and ground cinnamon (if using).
2. **Blend Until Smooth:**
   - Blend on high until smooth and creamy. If the smoothie is too thick, add more almond milk a little at a time until you reach your desired consistency.
3. **Add Sweetener (Optional):**
   - Taste the smoothie and add honey or maple syrup if you prefer a sweeter smoothie. Blend again to combine.
4. **Add Oats (Optional):**
   - If you're adding rolled oats for extra fiber and texture, add them to the blender and blend until smooth.
5. **Serve:**
   - Pour the smoothie into a glass and enjoy immediately.

Tips:

- For a thicker smoothie, use more frozen strawberries or add a few ice cubes.
- If you prefer a more dessert-like flavor, you can add a small handful of crushed graham crackers on top for a shortcake-like crunch.

This Healthy Strawberry Shortcake Smoothie provides the delightful taste of strawberry shortcake in a nutritious, refreshing format. It's perfect for breakfast, a snack, or even a light dessert!

Spiced Pumpkin Smoothie

Ingredients:

- 1/2 cup canned pumpkin puree (not pumpkin pie filling)
- 1 banana (fresh or frozen)
- 1/2 cup Greek yogurt or non-dairy yogurt
- 1/2 cup unsweetened almond milk or any milk of your choice
- 1 tablespoon maple syrup or honey (adjust to taste)
- 1/2 teaspoon ground cinnamon
- 1/4 teaspoon ground nutmeg
- 1/4 teaspoon ground ginger
- A pinch of ground cloves (optional, for extra spice)
- 1/4 cup rolled oats (optional, for added fiber)
- Ice cubes (optional, for a thicker, colder smoothie)

Instructions:

1. **Blend Ingredients:**
   - In a blender, combine the pumpkin puree, banana, Greek yogurt, almond milk, maple syrup or honey, ground cinnamon, nutmeg, ginger, and cloves (if using).
2. **Blend Until Smooth:**
   - Blend on high until the mixture is smooth and creamy. If the smoothie is too thick, add a bit more milk. If using fresh banana and you want a colder smoothie, add a few ice cubes and blend again.
3. **Add Oats (Optional):**
   - If you're using rolled oats for added fiber and texture, add them to the blender and blend until smooth.
4. **Adjust Sweetness and Spice:**
   - Taste the smoothie and adjust the sweetness with more maple syrup or honey if needed. You can also add a bit more cinnamon or nutmeg if you prefer a spicier flavor.
5. **Serve:**
   - Pour the smoothie into a glass and enjoy immediately.

Tips:

- For a thicker texture, use frozen banana or add extra ice cubes.
- You can also top the smoothie with a sprinkle of cinnamon or a few chopped nuts for added texture and flavor.

This Spiced Pumpkin Smoothie is perfect for celebrating fall flavors and is a nutritious way to enjoy pumpkin outside of the traditional pie. It's great for breakfast, a snack, or even as a light dessert!

Blackberry Chia Seed Smoothie

Ingredients:

- 1 cup fresh or frozen blackberries
- 1 banana (fresh or frozen, for natural sweetness and creaminess)
- 1/2 cup Greek yogurt or non-dairy yogurt (for creaminess and protein)
- 1/2 cup almond milk or any milk of your choice
- 1 tablespoon chia seeds
- 1 tablespoon honey or maple syrup (optional, for added sweetness)
- 1/2 teaspoon vanilla extract (optional, for extra flavor)
- A handful of ice cubes (optional, if using fresh fruit or if you prefer a colder smoothie)

Instructions:

1. **Prepare Chia Seeds:**
   - If you have time, let the chia seeds soak in a little bit of water or milk for about 10-15 minutes before blending. This helps them expand and become gel-like, but it's not essential if you're short on time.
2. **Blend Ingredients:**
   - In a blender, combine the blackberries, banana, Greek yogurt, almond milk, and chia seeds.
3. **Blend Until Smooth:**
   - Blend on high until smooth and creamy. If the smoothie is too thick, add a bit more milk. If you're using fresh fruit and want a colder smoothie, add a handful of ice cubes and blend again.
4. **Adjust Sweetness (Optional):**
   - Taste the smoothie and add honey or maple syrup if you prefer it sweeter. Blend again to combine.
5. **Add Vanilla (Optional):**
   - For extra flavor, you can add a splash of vanilla extract and blend again.
6. **Serve:**
   - Pour the smoothie into a glass and enjoy immediately.

Tips:

- If you prefer a thicker smoothie, use frozen blackberries or additional ice cubes.
- For added texture and nutrition, you can sprinkle some extra chia seeds on top before serving.
- You can also add a handful of spinach or kale for a green smoothie variation without altering the flavor much.

This Blackberry Chia Seed Smoothie is not only delicious but also packed with antioxidants, fiber, and protein, making it a great option for breakfast or a refreshing snack!

Chocolate Avocado Pudding

Ingredients:

- 2 ripe avocados
- 1/4 cup unsweetened cocoa powder
- 1/4 cup pure maple syrup or honey (adjust to taste)
- 1/4 cup coconut milk (or any milk of your choice)
- 1 teaspoon vanilla extract
- A pinch of salt
- Optional: 1/4 cup melted dark chocolate (for extra richness)

Instructions:

1. **Prepare the Avocados:**
   - Cut the avocados in half, remove the pits, and scoop the flesh into a food processor or blender.
2. **Blend Ingredients:**
   - Add the cocoa powder, maple syrup or honey, coconut milk, vanilla extract, and a pinch of salt to the avocado.
   - Blend until completely smooth and creamy. You may need to stop and scrape down the sides of the blender or food processor to ensure everything is well combined.
3. **Adjust Sweetness and Flavor:**
   - Taste the pudding and adjust the sweetness or cocoa powder as needed. If you like a richer chocolate flavor, you can blend in the melted dark chocolate.
4. **Chill:**
   - Transfer the pudding to serving bowls and refrigerate for at least 30 minutes to allow it to firm up and the flavors to meld.
5. **Serve:**
   - Serve chilled. You can garnish with fresh berries, a dollop of coconut whipped cream, or a sprinkle of sea salt.

Tips:

- For a smoother texture, make sure the avocados are fully ripe and blend the mixture thoroughly.
- If the pudding is too thick, you can add a little more coconut milk to reach your desired consistency.
- You can also experiment with adding a splash of coffee or a bit of cinnamon for a unique flavor twist.

This Chocolate Avocado Pudding is a decadent yet healthy dessert option that satisfies chocolate cravings while providing beneficial fats and nutrients. Enjoy!

Vegan Ice Cream Base

Ingredients:

- 1 can (14 ounces) full-fat coconut milk (or use a blend of coconut milk and almond milk for a lighter version)
- 1/2 cup maple syrup, agave nectar, or another liquid sweetener (adjust to taste)
- 1 tablespoon vanilla extract
- 1/4 teaspoon salt

Instructions:

1. **Combine Ingredients:**
   - In a medium bowl, whisk together the coconut milk, maple syrup (or sweetener of your choice), vanilla extract, and salt until well combined.
2. **Chill:**
   - Refrigerate the mixture for at least 2 hours or until well chilled. This step helps to improve the texture of the ice cream.
3. **Churn:**
   - Pour the chilled mixture into an ice cream maker and churn according to the manufacturer's instructions. Typically, this takes about 20-30 minutes.
4. **Freeze:**
   - Once the mixture has thickened and resembles soft-serve ice cream, transfer it to an airtight container and freeze for at least 2-4 hours, or until firm.
5. **Serve:**
   - Scoop and enjoy your homemade vegan ice cream!

Tips for Flavor Variations:

- **Chocolate:** Add 1/2 cup of unsweetened cocoa powder or melted dark chocolate to the base before churning.
- **Fruit:** Blend in 1-2 cups of fresh or frozen fruit (like strawberries, mangoes, or blueberries) with the base mixture before churning.
- **Mint Chocolate Chip:** Add a few drops of peppermint extract and mix in dairy-free chocolate chips during the last few minutes of churning.
- **Coffee:** Stir in 1-2 tablespoons of instant coffee or espresso powder to the base mixture.

Without an Ice Cream Maker: If you don't have an ice cream maker, you can still make vegan ice cream:

1. **Freeze and Blend:** Pour the chilled mixture into a shallow dish and freeze until mostly firm. Stir every 30 minutes for the first 2 hours to break up ice crystals.
2. **Blend:** Once it's firm but still a bit soft, blend it in a food processor until smooth and creamy. Then, refreeze until fully set.

This vegan ice cream base provides a creamy, delicious canvas for a wide range of flavors and mix-ins, allowing you to create a variety of dairy-free ice creams right at home. Enjoy experimenting with your favorite combinations!

Mango Lassi

Ingredients:

- 1 cup fresh or frozen mango chunks
- 1 cup plain Greek yogurt or non-dairy yogurt
- 1/2 cup milk (dairy or plant-based, like almond or coconut milk)
- 2 tablespoons honey or maple syrup (adjust to taste)
- 1/4 teaspoon ground cardamom (optional, for a traditional flavor)
- A pinch of ground turmeric (optional, for color and a hint of flavor)
- Ice cubes (optional, for a chilled version)

Instructions:

1. **Blend Ingredients:**
   - In a blender, combine the mango chunks, Greek yogurt, milk, honey or maple syrup, and ground cardamom (if using). If you're using ice cubes, add them to the blender as well.
2. **Blend Until Smooth:**
   - Blend on high until the mixture is smooth and creamy. If the lassi is too thick, you can add a bit more milk to reach your desired consistency.
3. **Taste and Adjust:**
   - Taste the lassi and adjust the sweetness with more honey or maple syrup if needed. If you're using ground turmeric, add a pinch and blend again to incorporate it.
4. **Serve:**
   - Pour the Mango Lassi into glasses and serve immediately. You can garnish with a sprinkle of ground cardamom or a few mint leaves if desired.

Tips:

- **Mango:** If you're using fresh mango, make sure it's ripe for the best flavor. If using frozen mango, you might not need ice cubes.
- **Yogurt:** Greek yogurt makes for a creamier lassi, but you can use regular yogurt or a non-dairy alternative depending on your preference.
- **Spices:** Ground cardamom and turmeric are optional but can add a nice touch of traditional flavor.

This Mango Lassi is perfect as a refreshing beverage on a hot day or as a delightful complement to a spicy meal. Enjoy!

Beet Apple Smoothie

Ingredients:

- 1 small beet, peeled and chopped (or 1 cup pre-cooked beet chunks)
- 1 apple, cored and chopped (leave the skin on for extra fiber)
- 1/2 banana (fresh or frozen, for added creaminess and natural sweetness)
- 1/2 cup Greek yogurt or non-dairy yogurt (for creaminess)
- 1/2 cup unsweetened almond milk or any milk of your choice
- 1 tablespoon honey or maple syrup (optional, for added sweetness)
- 1/2 teaspoon ground ginger (optional, for a bit of spice)
- 1/4 teaspoon ground cinnamon (optional, for added flavor)
- Ice cubes (optional, for a chilled smoothie)

Instructions:

1. **Prepare the Beet:**
   - If you're using raw beets, peel and chop them into small pieces. For a quicker option, you can use pre-cooked or roasted beet chunks, which are often available in stores.
2. **Blend Ingredients:**
   - In a blender, combine the chopped beet, apple, banana, Greek yogurt, and almond milk.
3. **Blend Until Smooth:**
   - Blend on high until the mixture is smooth and creamy. If the smoothie is too thick, add a bit more milk to reach your desired consistency.
4. **Add Sweeteners and Spices:**
   - Taste the smoothie and add honey or maple syrup if you prefer a sweeter smoothie. You can also add ground ginger and cinnamon if desired. Blend again to incorporate these additions.
5. **Add Ice (Optional):**
   - If you're using fresh fruit and want a colder, thicker smoothie, add a handful of ice cubes and blend again until smooth.
6. **Serve:**
   - Pour the smoothie into a glass and enjoy immediately.

Tips:

- **Beets:** If you prefer a milder beet flavor, you can start with a smaller amount and adjust according to taste.
- **Banana:** Using a frozen banana will make the smoothie colder and creamier.
- **Sweeteners:** Adjust the sweetness to your liking, especially if you're using tart apples.

This Beet Apple Smoothie is a great way to incorporate more vegetables and fruits into your diet while enjoying a delicious and refreshing drink. The combination of beets and apples not only provides a beautiful color but also a wealth of nutrients. Enjoy!

Mint Chocolate Chip Smoothie

Ingredients:

- 1 cup fresh spinach or kale (for a green boost, optional)
- 1 banana (fresh or frozen, for creaminess)
- 1 cup unsweetened almond milk or any milk of your choice
- 1/2 cup Greek yogurt or non-dairy yogurt (for creaminess)
- 2 tablespoons cocoa powder or 1/4 cup dairy-free chocolate chips (for a rich chocolate flavor)
- 1/2 teaspoon peppermint extract (adjust to taste)
- 1 tablespoon maple syrup or honey (optional, for added sweetness)
- 1/4 cup mini chocolate chips (for garnish, optional)
- Ice cubes (optional, for a chilled smoothie)

Instructions:

1. **Blend Ingredients:**
    - In a blender, combine the banana, almond milk, Greek yogurt, cocoa powder or chocolate chips, and peppermint extract.
2. **Blend Until Smooth:**
    - Blend on high until the mixture is smooth and creamy. If the smoothie is too thick, you can add a bit more almond milk to reach your desired consistency.
3. **Adjust Sweetness and Mint Flavor:**
    - Taste the smoothie and add maple syrup or honey if you prefer it sweeter. Adjust the amount of peppermint extract to your taste. Blend again to combine.
4. **Add Ice (Optional):**
    - If you're using fresh banana and want a colder, thicker smoothie, add a handful of ice cubes and blend again until smooth.
5. **Serve:**
    - Pour the smoothie into a glass and sprinkle with mini chocolate chips on top if desired. Enjoy immediately.

Tips:

- **Mint Extract:** Start with a small amount of peppermint extract and add more to taste, as it can be quite strong.
- **Chocolate Chips:** If you're using chocolate chips, blending them in will give the smoothie a richer chocolate flavor. For a smoother texture, use cocoa powder instead.
- **Greens:** Adding spinach or kale is optional but provides a nutritional boost without altering the flavor much.

This Mint Chocolate Chip Smoothie is a refreshing, nutritious way to enjoy the classic mint-chocolate combination. It's perfect for breakfast, a snack, or even as a dessert!

Pineapple Mint Smoothie

Ingredients:

- 1 cup fresh or frozen pineapple chunks
- 1/2 cup Greek yogurt or non-dairy yogurt (for creaminess)
- 1/2 banana (fresh or frozen, for added creaminess and natural sweetness)
- 1/2 cup coconut water or unsweetened almond milk (or any liquid of your choice)
- 1 tablespoon honey or maple syrup (optional, for added sweetness)
- A handful of fresh mint leaves (about 10-12 leaves, adjust to taste)
- Ice cubes (optional, for a colder, thicker smoothie)

Instructions:

1. **Prepare Ingredients:**
    - If using fresh pineapple, peel and chop it into chunks. If using frozen pineapple, you can skip the ice cubes for a thicker smoothie.
2. **Blend Ingredients:**
    - In a blender, combine the pineapple chunks, Greek yogurt, banana, coconut water or almond milk, and fresh mint leaves.
3. **Blend Until Smooth:**
    - Blend on high until the mixture is smooth and creamy. If the smoothie is too thick, you can add a bit more coconut water or almond milk to reach your desired consistency.
4. **Adjust Sweetness:**
    - Taste the smoothie and add honey or maple syrup if you prefer a sweeter taste. Blend again to combine.
5. **Add Ice (Optional):**
    - If using fresh pineapple and you want a colder, thicker smoothie, add a handful of ice cubes and blend again until smooth.
6. **Serve:**
    - Pour the smoothie into a glass and enjoy immediately. You can garnish with a few extra mint leaves or a pineapple wedge if desired.

Tips:

- **Mint:** Adjust the amount of mint leaves based on your preference. Too much mint can be overpowering, so start with a smaller amount and taste as you go.
- **Coconut Water:** Coconut water adds a subtle flavor and extra hydration, but you can use any liquid you prefer.
- **Frozen Fruit:** Using frozen pineapple will make the smoothie thicker and colder. If using fresh pineapple, ice cubes can help achieve the same effect.

This Pineapple Mint Smoothie is a tropical, refreshing drink that's both delicious and revitalizing. It's perfect for a quick breakfast, a post-workout snack, or a cool treat on a hot day. Enjoy!

Creamy Avocado Cilantro Dressing

Ingredients:

- 1 ripe avocado
- 1/2 cup fresh cilantro leaves (packed)
- 1/4 cup Greek yogurt or non-dairy yogurt (for creaminess; you can also use sour cream)
- 1/4 cup water (or more, to adjust consistency)
- 2 tablespoons lime juice (about 1 lime)
- 1-2 cloves garlic (optional, for extra flavor)
- 1 tablespoon olive oil (optional, for extra richness)
- Salt and pepper to taste

Instructions:

1. **Prepare the Avocado:**
   - Cut the avocado in half, remove the pit, and scoop the flesh into a blender or food processor.
2. **Blend Ingredients:**
   - Add the cilantro leaves, Greek yogurt, water, lime juice, garlic (if using), and olive oil (if using) to the blender or food processor.
3. **Blend Until Smooth:**
   - Blend on high until the mixture is smooth and creamy. If the dressing is too thick, add more water a tablespoon at a time until you reach your desired consistency.
4. **Season:**
   - Taste the dressing and add salt and pepper to your preference. Blend again to combine.
5. **Serve or Store:**
   - Use the dressing immediately or transfer it to an airtight container. It can be stored in the refrigerator for up to 3-4 days.

Tips:

- **Adjusting Consistency:** If you prefer a thicker dressing, use less water. For a thinner consistency, add more water or a bit more yogurt.
- **Flavor Variations:** You can add a pinch of ground cumin or a small handful of chopped jalapeño for a spicier kick.
- **Sweetness:** If you like a touch of sweetness, you can add a teaspoon of honey or agave nectar.

This Creamy Avocado Cilantro Dressing is perfect for adding a creamy, tangy twist to salads, grain bowls, or as a dip for veggies. Enjoy its fresh and vibrant flavors!

Sweet Green Smoothie

Ingredients:

- 1 cup fresh spinach or kale (stems removed)
- 1 ripe banana (fresh or frozen, for natural sweetness and creaminess)
- 1/2 cup pineapple chunks (fresh or frozen, for a tropical flavor and added sweetness)
- 1/2 cup apple or pear (cored and chopped, for extra sweetness and flavor)
- 1/2 cup coconut water or unsweetened almond milk (or any liquid of your choice)
- 1 tablespoon chia seeds or flaxseeds (optional, for added fiber and omega-3s)
- 1 tablespoon honey or maple syrup (optional, for extra sweetness if needed)
- Ice cubes (optional, if you're using fresh fruit or want a colder smoothie)

Instructions:

1. **Prepare Ingredients:**
    - If you're using fresh pineapple and banana, peel and chop them. If using frozen fruit, you can skip the ice cubes.
2. **Blend Ingredients:**
    - In a blender, combine the spinach or kale, banana, pineapple chunks, apple or pear, and coconut water or almond milk.
3. **Blend Until Smooth:**
    - Blend on high until the mixture is smooth and creamy. If the smoothie is too thick, add a bit more liquid to reach your desired consistency.
4. **Add Optional Ingredients:**
    - If using, add chia seeds or flaxseeds to the blender and blend again until well combined.
5. **Adjust Sweetness:**
    - Taste the smoothie and add honey or maple syrup if you prefer it sweeter. Blend again to combine.
6. **Add Ice (Optional):**
    - If using fresh fruit and you want a colder, thicker smoothie, add a handful of ice cubes and blend again until smooth.
7. **Serve:**
    - Pour the smoothie into a glass and enjoy immediately.

Tips:

- **Greens:** Spinach has a milder flavor compared to kale, making it a good option for beginners. If you use kale, make sure to remove the tough stems for a smoother texture.
- **Frozen Fruit:** Using frozen pineapple and banana will make your smoothie colder and creamier.
- **Additional Flavors:** You can add a splash of lime juice or a small piece of ginger for an extra zing.

This Sweet Green Smoothie is a delicious way to enjoy a blend of fruits and vegetables, perfect for breakfast, a snack, or a post-workout boost. Enjoy the sweet and refreshing taste!

Apple Ginger Smoothie

Ingredients:

- 1 large apple, cored and chopped (leave the skin on for added fiber)
- 1/2 banana (fresh or frozen, for creaminess)
- 1/2 cup Greek yogurt or non-dairy yogurt (for creaminess)
- 1/2 cup unsweetened almond milk or any milk of your choice
- 1-2 teaspoons fresh ginger, peeled and grated (adjust to taste)
- 1 tablespoon honey or maple syrup (optional, for added sweetness)
- 1/2 teaspoon ground cinnamon (optional, for extra flavor)
- Ice cubes (optional, for a colder, thicker smoothie)

Instructions:

1. **Prepare Ingredients:**
   - Peel and grate the fresh ginger. If using frozen banana, you can skip the ice cubes.
2. **Blend Ingredients:**
   - In a blender, combine the chopped apple, banana, Greek yogurt, almond milk, and grated ginger.
3. **Blend Until Smooth:**
   - Blend on high until the mixture is smooth and creamy. If the smoothie is too thick, add a bit more milk to reach your desired consistency.
4. **Adjust Sweetness:**
   - Taste the smoothie and add honey or maple syrup if you prefer it sweeter. Blend again to combine.
5. **Add Cinnamon (Optional):**
   - For extra flavor, you can add ground cinnamon and blend again.
6. **Add Ice (Optional):**
   - If using fresh fruit and you want a colder, thicker smoothie, add a handful of ice cubes and blend again until smooth.
7. **Serve:**
   - Pour the smoothie into a glass and enjoy immediately.

Tips:

- **Ginger:** Fresh ginger has a strong flavor, so start with a small amount and adjust according to your taste preference.
- **Apple Varieties:** Any apple variety works, but sweeter apples like Fuji or Honeycrisp are great for a naturally sweeter smoothie.
- **Creaminess:** For a richer texture, you can add a tablespoon of nut butter or a bit more yogurt.

This Apple Ginger Smoothie is a refreshing way to enjoy the flavors of apple and ginger while getting a nutritional boost. It's perfect for a quick breakfast or a revitalizing snack!

Pear Spinach Smoothie

Ingredients:

- 1 ripe pear, cored and chopped (no need to peel if you prefer extra fiber)
- 1 cup fresh spinach leaves (packed)
- 1/2 banana (fresh or frozen, for creaminess)
- 1/2 cup Greek yogurt or non-dairy yogurt (for creaminess)
- 1/2 cup unsweetened almond milk or any milk of your choice
- 1 tablespoon honey or maple syrup (optional, for added sweetness)
- 1/4 teaspoon ground cinnamon (optional, for extra flavor)
- Ice cubes (optional, for a colder, thicker smoothie)

Instructions:

1. **Prepare Ingredients:**
   - Chop the pear into chunks. If using a fresh banana, you might want to add ice cubes if you prefer a colder smoothie.
2. **Blend Ingredients:**
   - In a blender, combine the chopped pear, spinach leaves, banana, Greek yogurt, and almond milk.
3. **Blend Until Smooth:**
   - Blend on high until the mixture is smooth and creamy. If the smoothie is too thick, add a bit more milk to achieve your desired consistency.
4. **Adjust Sweetness:**
   - Taste the smoothie and add honey or maple syrup if you'd like it sweeter. Blend again to combine.
5. **Add Cinnamon (Optional):**
   - For added flavor, you can blend in ground cinnamon.
6. **Add Ice (Optional):**
   - If using fresh fruit and you want a colder, thicker smoothie, add a handful of ice cubes and blend again until smooth.
7. **Serve:**
   - Pour the smoothie into a glass and enjoy immediately.

Tips:

- **Pear Ripeness:** Use a ripe pear for the best sweetness and flavor. If the pear isn't very sweet, you might need a bit more honey or maple syrup.
- **Spinach:** Fresh spinach works best, but you can use frozen spinach if that's what you have on hand. Just make sure to blend it well to avoid any chunks.
- **Additional Flavor:** If you like, you can add a splash of vanilla extract or a squeeze of lemon juice to brighten up the flavors.

This Pear Spinach Smoothie is a refreshing and wholesome way to enjoy a mix of fruits and greens. It's not only tasty but also packed with nutrients, making it a great choice for a healthful and satisfying smoothie.

Creamy Zucchini Soup

Ingredients:

- 4 medium zucchinis, chopped
- 1 large onion, chopped
- 2 cloves garlic, minced
- 1 tablespoon olive oil
- 4 cups vegetable broth (or chicken broth)
- 1 cup coconut milk or heavy cream (for creaminess)
- 1 teaspoon dried thyme or basil (or 1 tablespoon fresh)
- Salt and pepper to taste
- Optional: 1-2 tablespoons nutritional yeast (for a cheesy flavor)
- Optional: Fresh herbs for garnish (like parsley or basil)

Instructions:

1. **Sauté Vegetables:**
   - In a large pot, heat the olive oil over medium heat. Add the chopped onion and cook until it becomes translucent, about 5 minutes.
   - Add the minced garlic and cook for another 1-2 minutes until fragrant.
2. **Cook Zucchini:**
   - Add the chopped zucchini to the pot and cook for about 5 minutes, stirring occasionally, until the zucchini starts to soften.
3. **Add Broth and Simmer:**
   - Pour in the vegetable broth and bring to a boil. Reduce the heat and let it simmer for about 15 minutes, or until the zucchini is tender.
4. **Blend Soup:**
   - Using an immersion blender, blend the soup directly in the pot until it's smooth and creamy. Alternatively, you can transfer the soup in batches to a blender and blend until smooth. Be careful with hot liquids!
5. **Add Creaminess:**
   - Return the blended soup to the pot (if using a blender). Stir in the coconut milk or heavy cream. Add the dried thyme or basil, and season with salt and pepper to taste.
6. **Heat Through:**
   - Heat the soup over low heat for another 5 minutes, allowing the flavors to meld. If you're using nutritional yeast, stir it in at this point.
7. **Serve:**
   - Ladle the soup into bowls and garnish with fresh herbs if desired. Serve hot.

Tips:

- **Texture:** For a chunkier texture, you can blend only half of the soup and leave the rest as is.
- **Flavor Boost:** Add a squeeze of lemon juice for a touch of brightness.
- **Cream Alternatives:** If you prefer a lighter version, you can use a dairy-free cream alternative or just skip the cream altogether.

This Creamy Zucchini Soup is comforting and versatile, making it a great option for a quick weeknight dinner or a soothing lunch. Enjoy its creamy texture and delicate flavor!

Tomato Avocado Salsa

Ingredients:

- 3-4 ripe tomatoes, diced
- 1 ripe avocado, diced
- 1/4 cup red onion, finely chopped
- 1/4 cup fresh cilantro leaves, chopped
- 1 jalapeño or serrano pepper, seeded and finely chopped (optional, for heat)
- 1-2 tablespoons lime juice (about 1 lime)
- 1 tablespoon olive oil (optional, for richness)
- Salt and pepper to taste

Instructions:

1. **Prepare Ingredients:**
    - Dice the tomatoes and avocado into bite-sized pieces. Finely chop the red onion and cilantro. If using, seed and finely chop the jalapeño or serrano pepper.
2. **Combine Ingredients:**
    - In a medium bowl, gently combine the diced tomatoes, avocado, red onion, cilantro, and chopped pepper (if using).
3. **Season:**
    - Drizzle with lime juice and olive oil (if using). Season with salt and pepper to taste.
4. **Mix Gently:**
    - Gently stir the salsa to combine all ingredients, being careful not to mash the avocado.
5. **Serve:**
    - Serve immediately or chill in the refrigerator for up to 1 hour to allow the flavors to meld.

Tips:

- **Avocado:** If you're making the salsa ahead of time, the avocado can brown quickly. To slow this down, add the avocado just before serving.
- **Heat Level:** Adjust the amount of jalapeño or serrano pepper based on your heat preference. For a milder salsa, you can omit the pepper altogether.
- **Extra Flavor:** For additional flavor, you can add a pinch of ground cumin or a splash of red wine vinegar.

This Tomato Avocado Salsa is a versatile and flavorful addition to any meal. Its creamy and tangy profile makes it a great complement to a variety of dishes. Enjoy!

Raspberry Lemon Smoothie

Ingredients:

- 1 cup fresh or frozen raspberries
- 1 banana (fresh or frozen, for creaminess and natural sweetness)
- 1/2 cup Greek yogurt or non-dairy yogurt (for creaminess)
- 1/2 cup almond milk or any milk of your choice
- 1 tablespoon honey or maple syrup (optional, for extra sweetness)
- 1 tablespoon lemon juice (about 1/2 lemon)
- 1 teaspoon lemon zest (optional, for extra lemon flavor)
- Ice cubes (optional, for a colder, thicker smoothie)

Instructions:

1. **Prepare Ingredients:**
    - If using fresh raspberries, you can add ice cubes for a thicker smoothie. If using frozen raspberries, you can skip the ice.
2. **Blend Ingredients:**
    - In a blender, combine the raspberries, banana, Greek yogurt, almond milk, lemon juice, and lemon zest (if using).
3. **Blend Until Smooth:**
    - Blend on high until the mixture is smooth and creamy. If the smoothie is too thick, add a bit more almond milk to reach your desired consistency.
4. **Adjust Sweetness:**
    - Taste the smoothie and add honey or maple syrup if you prefer it sweeter. Blend again to combine.
5. **Add Ice (Optional):**
    - If using fresh fruit and you want a colder, thicker smoothie, add a handful of ice cubes and blend again until smooth.
6. **Serve:**
    - Pour the smoothie into a glass and enjoy immediately.

Tips:

- **Sweetness:** Adjust the sweetness based on your taste and the tartness of the raspberries. Frozen raspberries tend to be sweeter than fresh ones.
- **Lemon Zest:** Adding lemon zest enhances the lemon flavor and adds a nice aroma. If you prefer a milder lemon taste, you can skip it.
- **Creaminess:** For a richer texture, you can use full-fat Greek yogurt or add a bit of avocado.

This Raspberry Lemon Smoothie is not only delicious but also packed with antioxidants and vitamin C. It's a refreshing way to enjoy a nutritious drink that's both tangy and sweet. Enjoy!

Cucumber Melon Smoothie

Ingredients:

- 1 cup cubed cantaloupe or honeydew melon (fresh or frozen)
- 1/2 cucumber, peeled and chopped
- 1/2 banana (fresh or frozen, for creaminess)
- 1/2 cup Greek yogurt or non-dairy yogurt (for creaminess)
- 1/2 cup coconut water or unsweetened almond milk (or any liquid of your choice)
- 1 tablespoon honey or maple syrup (optional, for added sweetness)
- A few fresh mint leaves (optional, for added freshness)
- Ice cubes (optional, if using fresh melon and you want a colder smoothie)

Instructions:

1. **Prepare Ingredients:**
    - Peel and chop the cucumber. If using fresh melon, cube it into chunks. If using frozen melon, you can skip the ice cubes.
2. **Blend Ingredients:**
    - In a blender, combine the melon, cucumber, banana, Greek yogurt, and coconut water or almond milk.
3. **Blend Until Smooth:**
    - Blend on high until the mixture is smooth and creamy. If the smoothie is too thick, add a bit more coconut water or almond milk to reach your desired consistency.
4. **Adjust Sweetness:**
    - Taste the smoothie and add honey or maple syrup if you prefer it sweeter. Blend again to combine.
5. **Add Mint (Optional):**
    - For a refreshing twist, add a few fresh mint leaves to the blender and blend again.
6. **Add Ice (Optional):**
    - If using fresh melon and you want a colder, thicker smoothie, add a handful of ice cubes and blend again until smooth.
7. **Serve:**
    - Pour the smoothie into a glass and enjoy immediately.

Tips:

- **Cucumber:** For a milder flavor, you can use a seedless cucumber or remove the seeds from a regular cucumber.
- **Melon:** Cantaloupe and honeydew are both great options. Choose based on your preference or what you have on hand.
- **Mint:** Fresh mint adds a nice touch of flavor, but you can omit it if you prefer a more straightforward smoothie.

This Cucumber Melon Smoothie is a delightful and hydrating option that's perfect for staying cool and refreshed. Enjoy its light and fresh flavors!

Peanut Butter Banana Protein Shake

Ingredients:

- 1 ripe banana (fresh or frozen)
- 2 tablespoons peanut butter (or any nut butter of your choice)
- 1 scoop protein powder (vanilla or unflavored works best)
- 1 cup milk of your choice (dairy, almond, soy, etc.)
- 1/2 cup Greek yogurt or non-dairy yogurt (for added creaminess and protein)
- 1 tablespoon honey or maple syrup (optional, for extra sweetness)
- 1/4 teaspoon vanilla extract (optional, for extra flavor)
- Ice cubes (optional, for a colder, thicker shake)

Instructions:

1. **Prepare Ingredients:**
   - If using a fresh banana, you can add ice cubes to make the shake colder and thicker. If using a frozen banana, you can skip the ice.
2. **Blend Ingredients:**
   - In a blender, combine the banana, peanut butter, protein powder, milk, Greek yogurt, and vanilla extract (if using).
3. **Blend Until Smooth:**
   - Blend on high until the mixture is smooth and creamy. If the shake is too thick, add a bit more milk to reach your desired consistency.
4. **Adjust Sweetness:**
   - Taste the shake and add honey or maple syrup if you prefer it sweeter. Blend again to combine.
5. **Add Ice (Optional):**
   - If you're using fresh banana and want a colder, thicker shake, add a handful of ice cubes and blend again until smooth.
6. **Serve:**
   - Pour the shake into a glass and enjoy immediately.

Tips:

- **Protein Powder:** Choose a protein powder that fits your dietary preferences, such as whey, casein, or plant-based options like pea or hemp protein.
- **Nut Butter:** You can substitute peanut butter with other nut butters like almond or cashew butter for a different flavor.
- **Creaminess:** For a richer shake, use full-fat Greek yogurt or add a tablespoon of chia seeds.

This Peanut Butter Banana Protein Shake is not only delicious but also packed with protein and healthy fats, making it a great option for a satisfying and nutritious drink. Enjoy!

Cauliflower Rice

Ingredients:

- 1 large head of cauliflower (or about 4 cups of cauliflower florets)
- 1-2 tablespoons olive oil or coconut oil (for sautéing)
- Salt and pepper to taste
- Optional: 1-2 cloves garlic, minced (for added flavor)
- Optional: Fresh herbs (like parsley or cilantro) for garnish

Instructions:

1. **Prepare Cauliflower:**
   - Remove the leaves and stem from the cauliflower head. Cut the cauliflower into florets.
2. **Rice the Cauliflower:**
   - **Food Processor Method:** Place the cauliflower florets into a food processor in batches. Pulse until the cauliflower resembles rice grains. Be careful not to over-process, or you'll end up with cauliflower mush.
   - **Box Grater Method:** Alternatively, you can use a box grater to grate the cauliflower florets into rice-sized pieces.
3. **Cook Cauliflower Rice:**
   - **Sautéing:** Heat olive oil or coconut oil in a large skillet over medium heat. Add the cauliflower rice and cook for about 5-7 minutes, stirring occasionally, until it's tender and slightly golden. If using garlic, add it to the skillet and sauté for the last minute of cooking.
   - **Steaming:** For a lighter option, you can steam the cauliflower rice. Place it in a steamer basket over boiling water and steam for about 5 minutes, or until tender.
4. **Season:**
   - Season with salt and pepper to taste. You can also add other seasonings or fresh herbs as desired.
5. **Serve:**
   - Serve the cauliflower rice as a base for stir-fries, grain bowls, or alongside your favorite protein and vegetables. It can also be used as a side dish in place of traditional rice.

Tips:

- **Texture:** To avoid mushy cauliflower rice, be sure not to overcook it. It should be tender but still have a bit of texture.
- **Batch Cooking:** Cauliflower rice can be made ahead of time and stored in the refrigerator for up to 4 days. You can also freeze it for up to 1 month. To freeze, spread the cooked or uncooked cauliflower rice on a baking sheet and freeze in a single layer. Transfer to a freezer-safe bag or container.

Cauliflower rice is a great way to incorporate more vegetables into your diet while still enjoying the texture and versatility of rice. Enjoy experimenting with it in your favorite recipes!

Cilantro Avocado Smoothie

Ingredients:

- 1 ripe avocado
- 1/2 cup fresh cilantro leaves (packed)
- 1/2 cup Greek yogurt or non-dairy yogurt (for creaminess)
- 1 cup unsweetened almond milk or any milk of your choice
- 1 tablespoon lime juice (about 1/2 lime)
- 1 tablespoon honey or agave syrup (optional, for added sweetness)
- 1/2 cup ice cubes (optional, for a colder, thicker smoothie)
- Optional: 1/2 cup spinach or kale (for extra greens)

Instructions:

1. **Prepare Ingredients:**
   - Cut the avocado in half, remove the pit, and scoop the flesh into a blender.
   - If using fresh cilantro, rinse and pat dry. If you're adding spinach or kale, rinse and remove any tough stems.
2. **Blend Ingredients:**
   - Add the cilantro leaves, Greek yogurt, almond milk, lime juice, and honey or agave syrup (if using) to the blender.
3. **Blend Until Smooth:**
   - Blend on high until the mixture is smooth and creamy. If the smoothie is too thick, add a bit more almond milk to reach your desired consistency.
4. **Add Ice (Optional):**
   - If you're using fresh ingredients and want a colder, thicker smoothie, add a handful of ice cubes and blend again until smooth.
5. **Serve:**
   - Pour the smoothie into a glass and enjoy immediately.

Tips:

- **Avocado:** Use a ripe avocado for the best creaminess and flavor. If the avocado is not ripe enough, it may not blend as smoothly.
- **Sweetness:** Adjust the sweetness with honey or agave syrup according to your taste. If you prefer a more savory smoothie, you can skip the sweetener.
- **Herbs:** Cilantro adds a distinctive flavor. If you're not a fan of cilantro, you can use parsley as an alternative.

This Cilantro Avocado Smoothie is a refreshing and nutrient-rich option that offers a unique twist on traditional smoothies. Enjoy its creamy texture and fresh, herbaceous flavor!

Green Apple Kale Smoothie

Ingredients:

- 1 large green apple, cored and chopped (leave the skin on for extra fiber)
- 1 cup fresh kale leaves (stems removed)
- 1/2 banana (fresh or frozen, for creaminess)
- 1/2 cup Greek yogurt or non-dairy yogurt (for creaminess)
- 1/2 cup unsweetened almond milk or any milk of your choice
- 1 tablespoon lemon juice (about 1/2 lemon)
- 1 tablespoon honey or maple syrup (optional, for added sweetness)
- 1/2 cup ice cubes (optional, for a colder, thicker smoothie)

Instructions:

1. **Prepare Ingredients:**
    - Core and chop the green apple into chunks. If using a fresh banana, you can add ice cubes for a thicker smoothie. If using a frozen banana, you can skip the ice.
2. **Blend Ingredients:**
    - In a blender, combine the chopped green apple, kale leaves, banana, Greek yogurt, almond milk, and lemon juice.
3. **Blend Until Smooth:**
    - Blend on high until the mixture is smooth and creamy. If the smoothie is too thick, add a bit more almond milk to reach your desired consistency.
4. **Adjust Sweetness:**
    - Taste the smoothie and add honey or maple syrup if you prefer it sweeter. Blend again to combine.
5. **Add Ice (Optional):**
    - If using fresh fruit and you want a colder, thicker smoothie, add a handful of ice cubes and blend again until smooth.
6. **Serve:**
    - Pour the smoothie into a glass and enjoy immediately.

Tips:

- **Apple Variety:** Green apples like Granny Smith are ideal for their tart flavor, but you can use any variety you prefer.
- **Kale:** Fresh kale works best. If using pre-cut kale, make sure it's well-rinsed.
- **Creaminess:** For a richer texture, you can use full-fat Greek yogurt or add a tablespoon of chia seeds.

This Green Apple Kale Smoothie is a refreshing and healthful way to enjoy a nutrient-packed drink. Its combination of apple and kale provides a delicious balance of sweetness and earthiness, making it a great choice for a nutritious start to your day or a revitalizing snack.

Pumpkin Spice Smoothie

Ingredients:

- 1 cup canned pumpkin puree (not pumpkin pie filling)
- 1/2 banana (fresh or frozen, for creaminess)
- 1/2 cup Greek yogurt or non-dairy yogurt (for creaminess)
- 1/2 cup almond milk or any milk of your choice
- 1/4 cup oats (optional, for added texture and fiber)
- 1 tablespoon honey or maple syrup (optional, for extra sweetness)
- 1/2 teaspoon pumpkin pie spice (or a blend of cinnamon, nutmeg, and ginger)
- 1/4 teaspoon vanilla extract (optional, for extra flavor)
- 1/2 cup ice cubes (optional, for a colder, thicker smoothie)

Instructions:

1. **Prepare Ingredients:**
   - If using a fresh banana, you can add ice cubes for a thicker smoothie. If using a frozen banana, you can skip the ice.
2. **Blend Ingredients:**
   - In a blender, combine the pumpkin puree, banana, Greek yogurt, almond milk, oats (if using), honey or maple syrup (if using), pumpkin pie spice, and vanilla extract (if using).
3. **Blend Until Smooth:**
   - Blend on high until the mixture is smooth and creamy. If the smoothie is too thick, add a bit more almond milk to reach your desired consistency.
4. **Add Ice (Optional):**
   - If you're using fresh ingredients and want a colder, thicker smoothie, add a handful of ice cubes and blend again until smooth.
5. **Serve:**
   - Pour the smoothie into a glass and enjoy immediately.

Tips:

- **Pumpkin Puree:** Make sure to use plain canned pumpkin puree and not pumpkin pie filling, which contains added sugar and spices.
- **Spice Blend:** If you don't have pumpkin pie spice, you can make your own by combining 1/2 teaspoon cinnamon, 1/4 teaspoon nutmeg, and 1/4 teaspoon ginger.
- **Sweetness:** Adjust the sweetness to your taste by adding more honey or maple syrup if needed.

This Pumpkin Spice Smoothie is a cozy, nutritious way to enjoy the flavors of fall. It's creamy, spiced, and perfect for a seasonal treat!